A Se[   ]:
Building Bridges Between
Islam and the West

Wilton

December 1996

Wilton Park Paper 131

Report based on the 50th Anniversary Wilton Park Conference: 13 December 1996 on "A Sense of the Sacred: Building Bridges Between Islam and the West".

London: The Stationery Office

ISBN 0 11 701920 8
ISSN 0953 8542

Published by The Stationery Office and available from:

The Publications Centre
(mail, telephone and fax orders only)
PO Box 276, London SW8 5DT
General enquiries 0171 873 0011
Telephone orders 0171 873 9090
Fax orders 0171 873 8200

The Stationery Office Bookshops
59-60 Holborn Viaduct, London EC1A 2FD
temporary until mid 1998
(counter service and fax orders only)
Fax 0171 831 1326
68-69 Bull Street, Birmingham B4 6AD
0121 236 9696 Fax 0121 236 9699
33 Wine Street, Bristol BS1 2BQ
0117 926 4306 Fax 0117 929 4515
9-21 Princess Street, Manchester M60 8AS
0161 834 7201 Fax 0161 833 0634
16 Arthur Street, Belfast BT1 4GD
01232 238451 Fax 01232 235401
The Stationery Office Oriel Bookshop
The Friary, Cardiff CF1 4AA
01222 395548 Fax 01222 384347
71 Lothian Road, Edinburgh EH3 9AZ
(counter service only)

Customers in Scotland may
mail, telephone or fax their orders to:
Scottish Publications Sales
South Gyle Crescent, Edinburgh EH12 9EB
0131 228 4181 Fax 0131 622 7017

The Stationery Office's Accredited Agents
(see Yellow Pages)

and through good booksellers

Contents

1 Introduction

Colin Jennings and Robin Hart

Wilton Park celebrated its 50th Anniversary in 1996. To commemorate the event, a brief but special conference was held on 13 December, which was opened by His Royal Highness The Prince of Wales on the theme of 'A Sense of the Sacred: Building Bridges Between Islam and the West'. This Wilton Park Paper includes a summary of the points raised, the interventions by each of the six speakers, and a summary of points made in the discussion.

The conference focused on two linked issues: the need for a rediscovery of a Sense of the Sacred to guide man's handling of practical problems in the modern world, and the potential for improved links between the Christian and Islamic Worlds to help stimulate such a rediscovery.

A convincing case was made that, rather than being driven by purely materialistic factors, policy in such fields as healthcare, agriculture, urban planning and the environment should stem from the traditional values of the Abrahamic religions: respect for the natural order and man's place within it. This would represent a fundamental change of approach. The dangers of continuing on a path which allows scientific discoveries to become the main determinant of policy are all too apparent in developments such as the Bovine Spongiform Encephalopathy (BSE) 'Crisis'.

Finding ways of improving understanding between different religions and cultures is a key challenge. As standards of living and scientific development have accelerated over the centuries, the dangers of a uni-dimensional materialistic approach have become prevalent in the West. The Islamic World, on the other hand, continues to emphasise the timeless traditions of the natural order. The search for ways of effectively reintegrating the Sacred and the secular can benefit from a greater mutual understanding between the Christian and Islamic cultures, replacing the ignorance and prejudice which all too often currently prevail on either side. Such a search would itself help to build bridges between them.

It is vital that man rediscovers a spiritual basis for his conduct if he is to be more than a biological phenomenon on the 'bottom line' of the 'balance sheet' of life, with culture and art as optional extras. Although everybody has an innate spiritual awareness, many in the West refuse to admit it for fear of ridicule, in itself an indication of the loss of spiritual meaning in Western civilisation. The wisdom of the great religious traditions of Judaeo-Christendom and Islam, and the theories of Platonic metaphysics, which inspired Western philosophy and spirituality, have been neglected for centuries, with growing secularisation as people believed that happiness could be found through material well-being.

In Muslim communities a Sense of the Sacred still manifests itself in everyday life with prayer, fasting and the alms-tax, and through the strength of Islamic mysticism. Like religions of the East, Islam has retained a holistic view of the world, integrating the secular and the Sacred, and stressing the sacred nature of creation. At its 'authentic best' all Islamic traditions, in all areas of human effort, are rooted in the Qur'an.

But the Islamic World faces similar materialistic pressures to the West. There is therefore considerable potential for a process of learning and sharing between the two faiths. Neither need fear change: a willingness to repent and behave differently from hitherto is a feature of both faiths. A discussion of how each faith views and understands the natural world, in the light of scientific development, can be the meeting point where issues of real importance are discussed without either side needing to be defensive. At present, tolerance between Islam and Christianity has been eroded at the very time of increasing contact as peoples of different faiths and cultures live as neighbours.

Concerning the issue of the environment, the one-sided approach of the recent past fails to take account of its inter-relatedness with creation. The 1986 Assisi meeting brought together the great faiths and conservation bodies to consider how man cares for nature. An inter-faith model of man's relationship with nature, more recently put forward by the Orthodox Churches, recommends man's role as servant of creation rather than the more traditional models of master or steward. This servant model, building on the Islamic *khalifa* (the belief that God has appointed humanity as His Vice-Regent) and stressing the sacred nature of creation, (that nature is here for the glory of God, rather than here for us), demands a fundamental shift in our views.

Putting words into practice is more difficult. The Islamic Declaration, although adopted by a number of Muslim countries as the basis for their environmental law, still has potential for greater action. In Christianity there are many projects of practical stewardship, but more impact could be made through education and sensitive use of the land. A five-year project, 'Sacred Land', to be launched in the United Kingdom in 1997 with members of many faiths including Christianity and Islam, and major environment bodies, will re-open and create sacred sites across the country—this is a practical example of the Sense of the Sacred returning to the environment. Overall a sustainable balance in our relationship with nature is called for to safeguard the land, and its produce, for future generations.

In the field of healthcare, a Sense of the Sacred can be added to the current uni-dimensional approach with hospitals designed to reflect the wholeness of healing. Examples include the Marylebone Health Centre in London, the Bristol Cancer Help Centre, and the Inter-Faith Hospice in North London.

In architectural design and urban planning the material and spiritual can be combined to create buildings and communities in which people want to live, and which will have a lasting attraction.

Traditions in both the Islamic and Christian societies, which evolved from religious beliefs, should have a greater priority in determining medical practice, architectural developments and education policy. Building bridges between Islam and the West can, for example, be achieved by recruiting more Muslim teachers in British schools and establishing more teacher exchanges. There should be strengthened measures against religious discrimination at the work place. Adequate legal safeguards against incitement to religious hatred are also needed whilst safeguarding the right to freedom of expression. There is scope to build on a common commitment to justice and the rule of law, to helping the poor, to tolerance and understanding between societies.

The challenge is to avoid becoming enmeshed in political and economic processes which limit mankind's scope to realise spiritual and other ambitions. The goal for the Millennium must be for it to act as a catalyst for the rediscovery of a Sense of the Sacred as a 'rallying point' for all and, as part of that process, for encouraging greater links between Islam and the West.

2   Presentations

A Sense of The Sacred: Building Bridges Between Islam and the West

His Royal Highness THE PRINCE OF WALES

I am particularly pleased to help celebrate fifty years of Wilton Park's existence. Wilton Park has become an important and internationally respected institution for the study of international issues. I am sure that some of its reputation comes from its position in the lee of the South Downs; a wonderful place for reviving the spirit and inducing a sense of calm and quiet contemplation. I am not at all surprised that people should therefore want to come to Wilton Park to try to analyse and solve some of the world's more difficult problems. I wish the Centre all possible success for its next fifty years.

I hesitated a long time before suggesting that it might be worth trying to use this occasion to hold a seminar on a Sense of the Sacred and its relevance to the problem of understanding between the Islamic and Western worlds. I am only too aware that this is not a typical or, for some people, an easy or comfortable way of looking at what are often seen as intensely practical issues. But I am encouraged by the fact that, whenever I have summoned up my courage to speak about this subject in the past, even to groups of hard-headed, practical people like international financiers or property developers, it seems always to have struck an extraordinary chord, and captured a remarkable degree of attention. My belief is that in each one of us there is a distant echo of this Sense of the Sacred, but that the majority of us are terrified to admit its existence for fear of ridicule and abuse. This fear of ridicule, even to the extent of mentioning the name of God, is a classic indication of the loss of meaning in so-called 'Western' civilisation.

I start from the belief that Islamic civilisation at its best, like many of the religions of the East (Judaism, Hinduism, Jainism and Buddhism) has an important message for the West in the way it has retained a more integrated and integral view of the sanctity of the world around us. I feel that we in the West could be helped to rediscover those roots of our own understanding by an appreciation of the Islamic tradition's deep respect for the timeless traditions of the natural order. I believe that process could help in the task of bringing our two faiths closer together. It could also help us in the West to rethink, and for the better, our practical stewardship of man and his environment in fields like health-care, the natural environment and agriculture, as well as in architecture and urban planning. I want very briefly to explain why this might be so.

Modern materialism in my humble opinion is unbalanced and increasingly damaging in its long-term consequences. Yet nearly all the great religions of the world have held an integral view of the sanctity of the world. The Christian message with, for example, its deeply mystical and symbolic doctrine of the Incarnation, has been traditionally a message of the *unity* of the worlds of spirit and matter, and of God's manifestation in this world and in mankind. But during the last three centuries, in the Western World at least, a dangerous division has come into being in the way we perceive the world around us. Science has tried to assume a monopoly, even a tyranny, over our understanding. Religion and science have become separated, with the result, as William Wordsworth said, "Little we see in nature that is ours". Science has attempted to take over the natural world from God, with the result that it has fragmented the cosmos and relegated the Sacred to a separate, and secondary, compartment of our understanding, divorced from practical day to day existence.

We are only now beginning to gauge the disastrous results of this outlook. We in the Western World seem to have lost a sense of the *wholeness* of our environment, and of our immense and inalienable responsibility to the whole of creation. This has led to an increasing failure to appreciate or understand tradition, and the wisdom of our forebears accumulated over the centuries. Indeed, tradition is positively discriminated against, as if it was some socially unacceptable 'disease'.

In my view, a more holistic approach is needed in our contemporary world. Science has done the inestimable service of showing us a world much more complex than we ever imagined. But in its modern, materialist, one-dimensional form, it cannot explain everything. God is not merely the ultimate Newtonian mathematician or the mechanistic clockmaker. Francis Bacon said that "God will not produce miracles to convince those who cannot see the miracle of a growing blade of grass and falling rain". As science and technology have become increasingly separated from ethical, moral and sacred considerations, so have the implications of such a separation become more sombre and horrifying as we see, for example, in genetic manipulation, or in the consequences of the kind of (scientific) arrogance so blatant in the BSE 'scandal'.

I believe there is a growing sense of the danger of these materialist presumptions in our increasingly alienated and dissatisfied world. Some may say that the tide is, perhaps, beginning to turn, but I fear there are still large herds of conventional sacred cows blocking the path. Some scientists are slowly coming to realise the awe-inspiring complexity and *mystery* of the universe.

But there remains a need to rediscover the bridge between what the great faiths of the world have recognised as our inner and our outer worlds, our physical and our spiritual nature. That bridge is the expression of our humanity. It fulfils this role through the medium of traditional knowledge and art, which have civilised mankind and without which civilisation could not long be maintained. After centuries of neglect and cynicism the transcendental wisdom of the great religious traditions, including the Judaeo-Christian and the Islamic, and the metaphysics of the Platonic tradition which was such an important inspiration for Western philosophical and spiritual ideas is finally being rediscovered.

I have always felt that tradition is not a man-made element in our lives, but a God-given intuition of natural rhythms, of the fundamental harmony which emerges from the union of those paradoxical opposites which exist in every aspect of nature. Tradition reflects the timeless order of the cosmos, and anchors us into an awareness of the great mysteries of the universe so that, as Blake put it "we can see the World in a Grain of Sand and Eternity in an hour". That is why I believe Man is so much more than just a biological phenomenon resting on what we now seem to define as 'the bottom line' of the 'great balance sheet' of life, according to which art and culture are seen increasingly as optional extras in life. This view is so contrary, for example, to the outlook of the Muslim craftsman or artist, which was never concerned with display for its own sake, nor with progressing ever forward in his own ingenuity, but was content to submit a man's craft to God. That outlook reflects, the memorable passage in the Qur'an, "withersoever you turn there is the face of God and God is all embracing, all knowing". While appreciating that this essential innocence has been destroyed, and destroyed everywhere, I nevertheless believe that the survival of civilised values, as we have inherited them from our ancestors, depends on the corresponding survival in our hearts of that profound Sense of the Sacred and the spiritual.

Traditional religions, with their integral view of the universe, can help us in an important way to rediscover the importance of the integration of the secular and the sacred—as I tried to argue in my speech in Oxford in 1993 on Islam and the West. The danger of ignoring this essential aspect of our existence is not just spiritual or intellectual. It also lies at the heart of that great divide between the Islamic and Western Worlds over the place of materialism in our lives. In those instances where Islam chooses to reject Western materialism, this is not, in my view, only a political affectation or the result of envy or a sense of inferiority. Quite the opposite. And the danger that the gulf between the worlds of Islam and the other major Eastern religions on the one hand, and the West on the other, will grow ever wider and more un-bridgeable is real, unless we can explore together practical ways of integrating the Sacred and the secular in both our cultures in order to provide a true inspiration for the next century.

This rediscovery of an integrated view of the Sacred could also help us in areas of important practical activity. Whatever some scientists might say in medicine, the ruptures between religion and science, and between the material world and a Sense of the Sacred, have too often led to a blinkered approach to healthcare, and to a failure to understand the wholeness and manifest mystery of the healing process. Hospitals need to be conceived and, above all, designed to reflect the wholeness of healing if they are to help the process of recovery in a more complete way. Modern medicine remains too often a one-dimensional approach to illness which, however sophisticated and miraculous in some of its achievements, cannot of itself understand more than a fraction of what there is to know, and can still be enriched and enlightened by more traditional approaches. There are, I am glad to say, beacons of light seeking to integrate the modern and traditional approaches, such as the Marylebone Health Centre in London and the Bristol Cancer Help Centre.

Our environment has suffered beyond our worst nightmares, in part because of a one-sided approach to economic development which, until very recently, failed to take account of the inter-relatedness of creation. Little thought was given to the importance of finding that sustainable balance which worked within the grain of nature and understood the vital necessity of setting and respecting *limits*. This, for example, is why protection of our environment is a relatively recent concern, and why organic and sustainable farming are so important if we are to use the land in a way which will safeguard its ability to nourish future generations.

A third area in which this separation of the material and spiritual has had dramatic consequences is architecture. I believe this separation lies at the heart of the failure of so much modern architecture to understand the essential *spiritual* quality and the traditional principles that reflect a cosmic harmony, from which come buildings with which people feel comfortable and in which they want to live. That is why I started my own small Institute of Architecture some five years ago. Titus Buckhardt wrote "It is the nature of art to rejoice the soul, but not every art possesses a spiritual dimension". We see this spirituality in *traditional* Christian architecture which, incidentally, was also inspired by a far more profound symbolic awareness than could ever be imagined by those who categorise such architecture as a question of mere style. This spiritual dimension also infuses the intricate geometric and arabesque patterns of Islamic art and architecture, which are ultimately a manifestation of Divine Unity, which in turn is the central message of the Qur'an. The Prophet Mohammed himself is believed to have said "God is beautiful and He loves beauty".

Urban planning is also important. The great historian, Ibn Khaldun, understood that the intimate relationship between city life and spiritual tranquillity was an essential basis for civilisation. Can we ever again return to such harmony in our cities? Ibn Khaldun also wrote "as civilisations decay, so do the crafts".

All these principles are in essence a battle for preserving sacred values. It is a battle to restore an understanding of the spiritual integrity of our lives, and for reintegrating what the modern world has fragmented. Islamic culture in its traditional form has striven to preserve this integrated spiritual view of the world in a way we have not seen fit to do in recent generations in the West. There is much we can share with that Islamic

World view in this respect, and much in that world view which can help us to understand the shared and timeless elements in our two faiths. In that common endeavour both our modern societies, Islamic and Western, can learn afresh the traditional views of life common to our religions, as well as the sacred responsibilities we have for the care and stewardship of the world around us.

In my Oxford speech in 1993 I argued for a much greater effort to be made to encourage understanding between the Islamic and Western Worlds. My firm belief in the importance of that process has not changed. The harm that will be done to both cultures if ignorance and prejudice persist, or grow, will be incalculable. There are many ways in which this understanding and appreciation can be built. But even if we begin with a simple understanding of the Sacred, which permeates every aspect of our world, there is the potential for establishing new and valuable links between Islamic civilisation and the West. Perhaps, for instance, we could begin by having more Muslim teachers in British schools, or by encouraging exchanges of teachers. Everywhere in the world people are seemingly wanting to learn English. But in the West, in turn, we need to be taught by Islamic teachers how to learn once again with our hearts, as well as our heads.

The approaching Millennium may be the ideal catalyst for helping to explore and stimulate these links, and I hope we shall not ignore the opportunity this gives us to rediscover the spiritual underpinning of our entire existence. For myself, I am convinced that we can no longer afford, for the health and sustainability of a civilised existence, to ignore these timeless features of our world. A Sense of the Sacred can, I believe, help provide the basis for developing a new relationship of understanding which can only enhance the relations between our two faiths, and indeed between all faiths, for the benefit of our children and future generations.

Islamic Spirituality: A Way of Regarding the World

Professor Dr Annemarie Schimmel

When I was teaching at the University at Ankara in the Faculty of Islamic Theology, I tried one day to introduce my students to Rudolf Otto's description of the Sacred as manifesting itself in the *Mysterium tremendum* and the *Mysterium fascinans*, that is in the mystery that inspires awe, and even fear, and the mystery that radiates beauty and love. One of my Muslim students got up and said "Oh, that's nothing new! We have known that for the last thousand and odd years because we recognise God's manifestation in His two aspects: in His *Jalàl*, His tremendous power and might, and in His *Jamàl*, His unending beauty and love".

I think that it was at this point that I was inspired to turn my interest to the problem of the Sacred, or the Holy, and especially the concept of God in the Islamic World, as it has been expressed so clearly in the Qur'an by orthodox Muslims and by mystics. The Sufis of Yore in Iraq, in Iran, in Egypt and wherever they might be, knew that this whole world is the place where we can see the *manifestations* of the Divine, though not the Divine itself. The Divine is a 'vast desert', undescribable, as Meister Eckhart (ob. 1328) would say in his German sermons. It is the absolutely unattainable, unreachable; "the views do not reach him" as the Qur'an says (Sura 6,103). And yet the Muslims also knew that this invisible and incomprehensible Divine power manifests itself through signs. Did not the Qur'an state that God promises to show His signs *ayatihi*, "in the horizons, that is in the created world and in the souls of mankind?" (Sura 41,53). This is, to the Sufi understanding, a safe way of approaching the Sacred to a certain extent. For we can never understand, not even approach the Sacred because it is the *Deus nudus*, the 'naked God', who cannot be conceived or described. What we can grasp are only the garments that hide Him, as Mawlana Rumi, the greatest Persian mystical poet, (ob. 1273) says in his verse "*bi-giz dàman-i lutfash ki na-gahàn be-gurizad"* ("O grasp the hem of His kindness, for suddenly he will flee").

It is the attempt of mankind to touch just a little piece of the 'garments of God', which may help us to understand at least a tiny fragment of His Greatness. The early Sufis, like Rabia of Basra (ob 801) saw the world as something ephemeral, "Whatever is in it will pass" (Sura 28,88), but they tried to discover God's signs "in the horizons". Great Egyptian mystical thinkers like Dhu'n-Nun, listened, for the first time, to the silent hymns of all things created (and the Qur'an has stated that everything was created to worship God). They were able, in their meditations, to understand not only the song of the birds but also the rushing of the waters and the whispering of the wind; for there is a sign in everything to show us the way to the sphere of the Sacred.

This idea underlies one of the most important aspects of Islamic mysticism, of Islamic spirituality and has been reflected in numerous stories. For instance when Mawlana Rumi, in his *Mathnawi*, speaks of the little ants who wandered around a beautifully illuminated manuscript of the Qur'an. The first ant said "Oh look, what the pen can do!" The next said "No, it's the hand", and the third one said "It's the arm". So they tried to find who was the originator of the marvellous calligraphy and decoration on which they were walking, and finally they thought it must be the human mind. But Rumi concludes the story by saying "These poor things—they could not see that there is one source beyond all of their movements, a source that is higher than our understanding".

I think sometimes we modern people are in a position similar to that of the ants who do not understand that there is a supernatural (if I can use this word), a Sacred, a Holy source to all our movements. But I also think that out of this attitude of the Muslims, the feeling emerges that *al-mulk lillàh*, "The Kingdom (everything created) belongs to God". The philosopher-poet Muhammad Iqbal (ob. 1938) warned people not to forget this idea because, if the world belongs to God then it is the duty of man,

12

His servant, to work in it, embellish it, and to elaborate the possibilities which God set before him. "Don't ruin the world after it has been set straight" (Sura 7,56). Iqbal takes up this idea and admonishes humankind to keep this world in the best possible shape, for man is, so to speak, a co-creator, a co-worker with God; he is responsible for everything he does and should transform the creation in the most beautiful way. For the mystic's true attitude is not to lean back and recede completely into one's inner life; there are periods of receding into loneliness and others of returning to 'the world' to implement what he has experienced in his silent dialogue with God.

I was recently in Bukhara for the celebrations of the memory of the great Sufi Baha'addin Naqshband (ob. 1389). One of his sentences was repeated "the hand at work but the heart close to the Divine Friend". Our Uzbek friends were extremely interested in this attitude towards life, and I think this sentence can teach us how to arrange our own life. The heart has always to be connected with the higher world, with the area of the uncreated realm of the Sacred. We have to see the work of God even in its smallest manifestation, and I would say that this holds true not only for our attitude to nature but also to our approach to the modern world with all its technical developments.

It is, as His Royal Highness pointed out, very typical of the Muslim attitude that a work of art or of technology is not primarily attributed to the one who has produced it, rather when admiring it one says *subhàn Allâh* ("praised be God!") because it is God who works through the artist, the inventor, and the architect. This attitude is, to my feeling and understanding, extremely important; we should learn from it and perhaps also try to imitate it.

Let me close my talk with a little story I always loved. I learnt it in Turkey. It is essentially a story that takes up the traditional idea that everything created praises God and this praise can be heard everywhere. And it is likewise an application of the thought that the heart should always be busy with remembering God. In a Turkish dervish lodge the master sent out his disciples to collect flowers to decorate the convent, with the understanding that the one who brought the most beautiful decoration would one day be his successor. Everyone arrived with marvellous arrangements. Only one dervish brought one little, dried-up flower. The master said "Why didn't you bring something better?" The dervish replied "Look! When I walked through the fields, I heard that all the flowers were engaged in praising God, and I didn't want to interrupt them. Only this one had finished its praise and so I brought it". And it was this dervish who eventually became the master's successor!

A Sense of the Sacred Among the Religions

The Rt Revd Dr Michael Nazir-Ali

There is an innate spiritual awareness among men and women. It is this which makes us aware of our destiny and it is this which provides the pattern for our interaction with the world. It is this which makes knowledge of God and of right and wrong possible. As the novelist William Golding put it "however unpromising the material may appear to be, hidden behind the darkness within the human person, is the light and truth of God".

Christianity and Islam are both aware of this 'God-dimension' in the human personality. Christianity speaks of this as the *imago Dei*, the image of God in us. Islam speaks of it more in the sense of *khilafa*, or stewardship, which has been entrusted to humanity. Stewardship is, indeed, a common and important theme in both the Bible and the Qur'an and reminds us immediately that our Sense of the Sacred is related to the sacredness of the world around us. In spite of the world's tiredness because of human greed and exploitation, there still lives, as Gerard Manley Hopkins saw "the dearest freshness deep down things". It is part of human stewardship to allow this freshness to appear and to renew creation.

The lawfulness and order of the universe, on which the whole of the scientific enterprise is based, led Professor Dawkins, in his recent Dimbleby lecture, to awe and wonder. It leads Muslims

14

and Christians to acknowledge a beneficent Creator who has not only created an ordered and wonderful world, but has given us the capacity to wonder at it, to discover more about it and to adapt it for our own purposes. Allama Iqbal refers to this last capacity in one of his Persian poems:

"You made the night, and I the lamp,
You the clay, and I the cup,
You—desert, mountain-peak and vale,
I flower-bed, park and orchard".

Both Islam and Christianity are inescapably missionary religions. But as they have spread to different cultures, at their best they have tried to conserve and to build on the traditions, world-views and customs which they have encountered. In Christianity, this process is signalled by the somewhat ugly term 'inculturation' and in Islam in the way *ada*, or custom, is recognised in the application and development of *Shariah*. Indeed it may not be an exaggeration to say that many peoples and cultures would have disappeared altogether if there had not been such conservation!

What then is the role of *Revelation*? Both religions emphasise its centrality and derive their essential character from it. We may say that *Revelation confirms* what we know through conscience and through our awareness of the Sacred in the world at large. It also corrects what has gone wrong in ourselves and in the world around us. Because both traditions believe in human freedom, *Revelation* can only be *persuasive*, never *co-ercive*. In Christianity, this is seen, for example, in the Gospel accounts of the sending out of the Twelve. If people receive the apostles, they should stay with them and preach the good news. If they are not received, they should 'shake the dust' from their feet and leave (for example, Matthew 10:13-14). The Qur'an (2:256) too, is aware that a response to God's *Revelation* of his will can never be forced *"La Ikraha fiddini"* ("there is no compulsion in matters of faith").

For three hundred years before the conversion of Constantine, Christianity had no political power and its message was spread within families, at the work place and in the markets. In both the Roman and the Persian empires, Christians were sometimes tolerated but often persecuted. It was much the same with the Prophet of Islam's early preaching. His followers were often persecuted and he was harassed and ridiculed by his opponents. It is worth remembering that some of the Prophet's leading followers sought refuge in the Christian kingdom of Ethiopia. They were given sanctuary there in recognition of much that was seen to be in common between the refugees and their Ethiopian hosts. Throughout the Prophet's lifetime, the dialogue with Jews and Christians continued and when he acquired temporal authority in Medina, the Constitution of Medina was promulgated. This recognised the citizenship, within an Islamic policy, not only of the Jews and Christians but also of the pagans.

It is a pity, therefore, that when Christians and Muslims consolidated their temporal power, they lost this earlier commitment to tolerance. Legal systems, such as the codes of Theodosius and Justinian, made dissent from orthodoxy much more difficult. The different codes of *Shariah*, too, restricted the role of people of other faiths within the House of Islam and made any departure from orthodoxy difficult, if not impossible.

In today's world, Christians and Muslims are in increasing contact with one another. It is important that they should learn to live with each other and with people of other faiths. To do this effectively, they need to recover their original traditions and then to relate them to contemporary problems. In the West, for example, we need increasing recognition that Muslims often understand themselves more in terms of faith than of race. It is good that measures are beginning to be taken against religious discrimination at the work place. We need also to make sure that there are adequate legal safeguards against incitement to religious hatred, while, at the same time, protecting the rights to freedom of expression.

There is considerable enthusiasm in the Islamic World to rediscover the roots of Islamic law and to use the principles of development inherent in Islamic jurisprudence. This is vitally important if new arrangements are to emerge which enable Muslims to live in harmony and friendship with people of other faiths.

Muslims and Christians both believe that God has revealed His will in a particular way. Such an understanding has, however, always to be related to the changing circumstances in which believers find themselves. Both believe that the law is summed up in our duty to love God with all our heart, soul and mind and our neighbour as ourselves. Let us make sure we do so.

As Maulana Jalaluddin Rumi, the famous Sufi poet has said:

"By love the bitter is made sweet, by love base metal turns to gold,
By love the dregs become clear, by love pains are healed,
By love the dead are raised, by love the King is made a slave!"

Science as a Meeting Ground Between the Two Faiths

Dr John Polkinghorne

One of the most important developments of our time is the meetings beginning to take place between world faiths. No longer are people of other religions strange people in far away places, but they are our neighbours. These encounters lead us to recognise that authentic spiritual experience and insight is preserved in each of these communities. We share a Sense of the Sacred. We also have things to learn from each other. Yet we are also aware of the differing, and sometimes clashing, accounts which the traditions give of the nature of Ultimate Reality. Each faith is the jealous guardian of its central tenets. Meaningful dialogue will have to start at the peripheries where encounter is least threatening to each side. I suggest that discussion of how each faith views and understands the physical world, particularly in the light of all that contemporary science can tell us of the pattern and history of the universe, provides a meeting point where the conversation can concern issues of real importance without leading to any temptation for either side to be defensive.

The Abrahamic faiths should find such an encounter particularly congenial. It is clear that we worship the same God, though we have different, and not completely compatible, things to say about the divine nature and self-revelation. Yet we agree that God is the Creator whose Mind and Will lies behind the stupendous history of the universe, a history which over fifteen billion years has displayed an astonishing fruitfulness, turning an initial ball of energy into the home of saints and scientists. That thought alone is enough to encourage our common Christian and Islamic belief that we live in a creation. We agree about the reality of the physical world and that there is a truth, God's truth, to be found out about it. We reject contemporary relativism's assertion that all we can achieve through scientific investigation is the formation of useful manners of speaking. Instead, we agree with those cosmologists who say, with what degree of seriousness it is hard to say, that science is privileged to participate in a reading of the mind of God, though we know that there is much more to the Mind of God than science will ever be able to discover.

That Christianity and Islam should have a positive attitude to scientific truth is scarcely surprising, since adherents of the two faiths played leading roles in the coming to birth of science itself in its recognisably modern form. Islamic thinkers preserved and developed the insights of Aristotle and other Greek thinkers, transmitting these ideas eventually to the Christian West where they were taken up and further explored. But the Abrahamic faiths knew something that the Greeks did not: that God is sovereignly free in the act of creation—no pre-existing realm of ideas constrains the Creator's choice of the pattern of creation. In consequence one must look to see what is the lawful nature of creation; it cannot be discovered by pure thought alone. This recognition of the need for observation and experiment was an indispensable prerequisite for true discovery, the great birthday present of the Abrahamic faiths to infant science for which their offspring ought to be everlastingly grateful. Believers from both traditions continue to contribute to the advance of science. I say that with some feeling since I was supervised for my Doctorate by the Nobel Prize winning Pakistani physicist, Abdus Salam. I would like to put on record my debt of gratitude to Abdus, who sadly died recently. From time to time we would discuss religious matters and we were both conscious of being engaged in a great human venture exploring the wonders of God's creation.

Together our two communities can witness to the signs of the Creator's Mind and Purpose which are disclosed in the ordered and fruitful universe we inhabit. The world is not full of objects labelled 'made by God'; the Creator is more subtle than that. Yet there are questions which arise from our scientific experience but which go beyond the narrow confines of what science permits itself to address. These deeper questions are certainly meaningful and necessary to ask, and I believe that religious traditions can provide coherent and intellectually satisfying answers to them.

Why is science possible at all? Why can we understand the physical universe so deeply and find such wonder in the understanding that is granted to us? Our powers of comprehension vastly exceed anything required for the evolutionary necessities of everyday survival. Our faiths both reply that it is because the world is a creation and we are creatures made in the image of our Creator. I find that a foundly satisfying insight. Why is the universe so special, its basic physical laws finely tuned to make carbon-based life possible, so that the coming-to-be of self-conscious life seems no accident but rather the realisation of a potentiality that was built into the physical fabric of the universe from the start? Together we reply again, because this is God's world, God's creation. I often give talks about these issues, and it is a frequent experience that Muslims in the audience will tell me how much they agree with what I have been saying. Of course, I welcome their support. We must make common cause in witnessing to our secular society that science, to many the grounding of secularity, points beyond itself to the God of all truth, including the truths of science.

We must make common cause also in seeking wisdom to make use of the discoveries of science in ways that are made for human flourishing and display a respect for the whole of creation. All advances in knowledge bring with them the potential for their good and bad use. The advice of experts is an indispensable input into wise-decision making but they possess no monopoly of wisdom. The insights of the great religious traditions are an equally indispensable resource in our search for just and sustainable policies.

On an occasion like this, I find myself thinking, with admiration and some wistfulness, of the later Middle Ages. Perhaps I have only to utter the names of Ibn Sina and Al Ghazali, of Moses Malmonides, of Thomas Aquinas, to indicate what I mean. There was a time when the great thinkers of the Abrahamic faiths interacted and influenced each other. Sadly that time passed, but we may hope and pray for its return. May God grant us all a passion for truth and a wonder and respect for the divine creation.

Sacred Land—the Rediscovery in Christianity and Islam of the Divine in Nature

Martin Palmer

The topic of this conference could not be more relevant for there seems to be a change in the flow of secularism and a revival of religion. Not all this is for the good, but in certain areas, it is of great significance.

For over ten years, my colleagues in the International Consultancy on Religion, Education and Culture (ICOREC) and I have worked as religious advisers to secular conservation and ecological organisations seeking to develop links between the teachings of the great faiths and environmental practice. In particular, we have run the World Wide Fund for Nature's

(WWF) programme on religion and conservation which was launched ten years ago at Assisi, when all the major faiths and the major environmental organisations met for the first time. This network is now called the alliance of Religions and Conservation. The WWF sponsored work with religions has resulted in over 120,000 practical religious environmental projects.

When I am asked "Well what exactly do you do?" I often talk about our role with WWF. I usually get one of two responses. The first is a look of total incomprehension and a sudden desire to find someone else to talk to! The other is the wit, the wag who says "What are you trying to do, Convert the Pandas?" The first is to say I am trying to convert them to Catholicism—then they will have so many babies they will never die out. The second is that I am trying to convert them to Anglicanism, so they will just never make up their minds to die out!

Behind this lies an important truth. For many, religion has retreated from the public scene and the great issues of today are seen as having no significance for religion, nor religion for the issues. To many in the West, the claim of Nietzsche that "God is dead" echoes and provides a reason for ignoring the spiritual and religious dimension of life.

But things are changing. The Assisi meeting of the great faiths and conservation bodies was one indicator of this. The WWF has come to realise that information and knowledge alone are failing to make any difference to how people treat the natural world. Simply knowing how many hectares of rain forest have been lost this year doesn't mean you have any reason for caring or for doing something about it. Knowledge without moral and spiritual framework carries with it no implicit ethics or morality. It was for this reason, the failure of knowledge and science, that WWF turned to the great faiths. In the end, how you treat and use and understand nature depends upon what you believe about yourself and your place within all life. Faith in science, in God, or in deities, conscious or otherwise, colours the world one sees as reality.

I want to examine what has happened since Assisi in 1986 in terms of the Christian and Islamic response. Let me be quite frank. When WWF asked the faiths to come to Assisi with basic outline statements on where they stood theologically, philosophically and pragmatically on the question of care for nature, few faiths had done any thinking about this. Some Christians had toyed with the issue for a decade or so but no major statement existed. Some Muslims had responded to the scientific data and had tried to raise ethical and spiritual issues but had been rebuffed.

Of all the statements at Assisi, the Islamic one was the most clear. It contained the only outright declaration of failure of any of the faiths, an honesty which won it much praise: "We often say Islam is a complete way of life, by which it is meant that our ethical system provides the bearings for all our actions. Yet our actions often undermine the very values we cherish. Often while working as scientists or technologists, economists or politicians, we act contrary to the environmental dictates of lslam".

So what are the dictates of Islam? The basis of Islamic understanding of our place in nature is summed up in three words: *tawheed* (the Unity of God signifying the unity of all He has created); *khalifa* (the belief that God has appointed humanity as His Vice-Regent, to rule the world justly and with compassion in His Name); and *akhirah* (the accountability we have as *khalifa* to God for how we tend His creation).

This vision is perhaps best summed up in the Hadith related by Imam Ahmad in his Musnad "If anyone plants a tree or sows a field, and men, beasts or birds eat from it, he should consider it as a charity on his part".

To be honest, the Christian Declaration at Assisi, prepared by the Vatican in consultation with the World Council of Churches, was a disappointment. It stumbled between two models, comfortable with neither. The first was the model of Master—of our having Dominion over creation. This was felt to be a rather 'heavy' model, and too tainted with association with the exploitative, dominance, patriarchal model which so many believe has helped produce the environmental crises we now face. Yet it addresses the reality of our immense power as a species. The question for Christians is how to make sense of this. The second model sought to soften the master model and was that of steward, one who looks after his Master's lands. It is close to *khalifa*, but not close enough. For essentially both Christian models at Assisi spoke of management, not of relationship.

It was not until in 1989 the Orthodox Churches spoke on this issue that an exciting model came forward, one the Orthodox have held for centuries but news to the Western Churches—it was that of priesthood, of a sacramental, sacral relationship with nature where we take upon ourselves the role of servants of creation, just as Christ, the all-powerful, emptied Himself and became human to serve us.

What is exciting about both the Islamic *tawheed*, *khalifa* and *akhirah* model and the Orthodox servant model is that they stress the sacred nature of creation. As His Royal Highness has said, Christianity through the incarnation brings together the spiritual and physical worlds as one unity. In Islam, there is a dynamic tension between those who would see God as entirely transcendent, and those who would also attribute an immanent quality to God. This means that we have to make a fundamental shift in our values. Nature is not here for us, but for the glory of God. That is the essential message of Orthodox Christianity and Islam.

But what does this mean? In Islam, the Islamic Declaration has been adopted by a number of Muslim countries, the first being Oman, as the basis for their environmental law. But worldwide, the Islamic potential for environmental action has yet to be realised. The launch of the Islamic Foundation for Ecology and Environmental Sciences (IFEES) is hopefully an indication of greater practical involvement by Muslims, though to date most IFEES funding has come from non-Muslim sources. It plans to set up an international centre of excellence in the United Kingdom, where Islamic teachings would be disseminated through practical land based projects such as land management which is organic, environmentally sensitive and manifests alternative economic models of development and sustainability.

I long for the day when Islam brings its concept of the sacredness of all that God creates to bear upon this modern urban world. And I look for not just the vast theories but the practical ideas as well, for example the insights of great jurists such as Izz ad-Din ibn Abd as-Salam, the 13th Century codifier of *Shariah*, who produced the world's first ever bill of legal rights of animals and nature.

In Christianity, there are literally tens of thousands of projects to date, ranging from education programmes to land use projects. But this still seems to make little impact on official teaching or practice as in for example the Church Commissioners and their lands.

The West has much to learn from the Islamic heritage on nature. We need the pragmatic thinking that lies behind the *Shariah*. How does one structure life in order to respect and maintain the sacred in our midst? Much contemporary Western so-called spiritual reflection on nature is very 'wishy-washy' and incapable of serious engagement with law, economics or science. Islam reminds us that faith can offer more. However, Christianity can offer Islam a timely reminder that words alone are not enough—action is also necessary. Together they offer to science moral, ethical and spiritual frameworks by which reality can be seen again and the Divine be discerned once more in nature.

Muslims and Christians as well as members of many other faiths and the major environment groups will join together in 1997 to launch 'Sacred Land', the re-hallowing of the environment of Britain. This five year project aims to put into practical use the teachings of the faiths on ecology by re-opening, rediscovering and creating anew, sacred sites across the length and breadth of Britain. One dimension will be to use what exists already from the great historic pilgrimage routes to the land surrounding mosques and churches. Practical programmes on ecology will take place. The second dimension is to create new special, sacred spaces ranging from quiet areas in school playgrounds to sacred gardens beside shopping malls.

In so doing, the Sense of Sacred within each faith will find expression in the very land we walk upon. In doing so, the faiths will show how seeing the world through sacred eyes, changes how you relate to it. *Khalifa* and servant join together with all that contemporary science can offer, to help us all live more sacred lives. Perhaps a renewed Sense of the Sacred in the mundane will turn out to be the greatest gift in this era of the two great faiths.

A Sense of The Sacred and the Unity of Man and Nature

Dr Fahan Nizami

From a Quranic perspective, let me begin by tentatively describing the Sense of the Sacred as a bridge between human beings and God. If that bridge is in disuse, the other bridges that we all wish to see functioning well between different peoples, different branches of learning, and so on, lose their usefulness. If we disown our Sense of the Sacred, we begin to regard the other bridges as constructions that are rather too fine, and idealistic to carry the weight of our differences. And a disused bridge can only serve as a boundary marker, not as a place of exchange.

Islamic civilisation is strong in the very direct relationship it enjoys with its scripture. At their authentic best, all Islamic traditions, in all domains of human effort, are rooted in the Qur'an and its embodiment in the custom and practice of the Prophet. A simple suffix changes the Arabic word for mosque to the word for university. And mosques are typically built into the market-place, often enough funded by the local traders. Thus, seeking learning, seeking one's livelihood and seeking nearness to God are intimately tied in with each other. The humblest acts of good neighbourliness or good citizenship can deserve the rank of worship. The Prophet describes clearing an obstacle from a road, even not annoying your neighbour, if done to please God, as acts of charity. The primary disciplines commanded by the Qur'an (prayer, fasting and the alms-tax) are the basis of normal (not especially religious) Muslim practice. Done with even a moderate degree of attentiveness, they raise one's awareness of the Sacred within the ordinary routines of life. In this way the link between worldly preoccupations and religious purpose is maintained.

Every human being, says the Qur'an, was, at the moment of ensoulment, asked "Am I not your Lord?" and each answered "Yes". And every human community was sent a Messenger, a communication of God's Will. This implies a primordial unity and equality among mankind; a rejection in principle of the idea that certain peoples are by nature confined to inferior darkness. According to the Qur'an all human beings must, in principle, be regarded as equally capable of the light, imperfect but perfectible. The Qur'an, uniquely, recognises the historic fact that there are different religious communities and envisages peaceful co-existence with these differences until God explains and reconciles them. In the meantime, the duty of God is to agree positively on what is common ground and compete, if compete we must, in good deeds.

That principle is the essential basis of the history of pluralism in Islamic civilisation, and one reason for its remarkably assimilative temperament, its capacity to learn as well as teach, to build upon existing cultures, as well as to mould and modify them. There are many examples in the sciences, in philosophy, in law and administration, in architecture and urban design, in the terminology and poetry of spiritual longing which indicates this assimilative temperament.

The Qur'an enabled a unification of secular and Sacred because its core message is the unity of God. God is the omnipotent and omnipresent Creator of all that is, living and non-living. The Qur'an tells us we were not present at the creation of the world, nor at our own: we did not spark ourselves into existence. Life and this world are given to us, and given by God. In many verses, in many contexts, the Qur'an reiterates the message: the Earth is given us to inhabit, therefore it is habitable by us. We should not need special apparatus to breathe the air or drink the water. Moreover, the Earth is beautiful as well as useful and filled with time—it is navigable and calculable; there is imagery of cattle and harvests, camels across the desert, and ships on the sea. But above all, it is intelligible. It is made to be reflected upon and understood. The phenomena of nature and of human experience and human history are called 'signs', the same term used for the verses of the Qur'an. The loss of those who do not reflect upon these signs with a religious seriousness, who refuse to inhabit and handle the world as a gift of God, is likened to the loss of the deaf and blind.

The Qur'an states that human beings were created to serve God. It follows that our Sense of the Sacred is the most important attribute of being human. Formal worship is just one, focused element of serving God. More broadly, service of God means a constant accountability to Him. Modern Western attitudes rebel against this feeling of accountability. They prefer instead an untrammelled tenure of life and of this planet. Such attitudes, let me stress, are no longer 'Western' in a geographical sense, only in point of cultural origin. Present-day Muslim societies are acquiring these attitudes at tremendous speed. Muslims are therefore as much in need of recovering the Sense of the Sacred as anybody else.

Accountability to God need not be a burden if we remember that being created to serve God, means being disposed in our deepest nature to do so. And God has so disposed us because accountability to Him, even when we dislike or reject it, perfects us, individually and collectively. Our Sense of the Sacred may then be understood as a great flow of energy, an enormous potential, to be loyal to God and, thereby, loyal to our own humanity. Conversely, blocking that flow of energy or diverting it is dangerous and detrimental to our humanity.

Without the Sense of the Sacred, human beings do, of course, still inhabit the earth, make use of it and of each other. But they enter upon their responsibility as human beings, even when well-intentioned, without sufficient grasp of their limitations, without sufficient consciousness of the ultimate outcome of their thoughts and actions. Consequently, relationships and structures and processes evolve in our affairs whose rationale is not to please God but, instead, to increase human power in the world. Value and worth are calculated in the short term: parents do not expect to have their tastes or mores shared by their own children, how then should they be expected to plan for their grand or even great-grand-children? We make things and build buildings to serve an immediate purpose profitably. We become unable to build something new that will remain magnificent and pleasing even as a ruin, hundreds of years from now. Indeed, even when we can imagine the distant consequences of our actions, we cannot translate that imagining into effective policy and obtain a consensus for it. We have good impulses but cannot enact them; we mean others well but find ourselves trapped in political and economic processes which do them harm. In other words, in the Qur'anic phrase, the wide earth becomes narrow for us. Though we have more power than could have been dreamt of a hundred years ago, we are unable to realise good from it, except in the material ease of the lives of a small portion of the world's people. And even that material ease must be secured in private estates within the unease and violence of uncivil cities.

His Royal Highness's plea to recover the Sense of the Sacred is a plea to respect and make reference to, even if we cannot fully revive, those of our traditions which evolved from our religious beliefs and cultures. Traditions in architecture, in husbandry, in medical practice, in educational institutions, and so on. This plea identifies the essential dimension lacking in collective modern life. It also locates a firm and secure foundation upon which bridges can be built towards the traditional societies, particularly of the Islamic World. As I have indicated, it is a plea that must and should be welcomed equally by Muslims and Westerners.

In response to that plea we have heard about the spiritual tradition in Islam, about the way scientific inquiry could combine religious commitment with a desire to understand the natural world, and the pluralism and tolerance exemplified in Islamic principles and practice—all these are openings on to a common ground. Let me also respond to His Royal Highness' plea by adding that there are common moral values whether related to the individual, family or society: commitment to justice and the rule of law, to public provision for the poor and the needy, and to tolerance and understanding. Muslims also share with Christians a belief in the same Emissaries of God, including Christ himself, and they honour and revere their lives and teachings. There is also the tradition of academic collaboration within the Islamic world between Muslims and non-Muslims, and the whole history of the transmission of learning to Europe. We even have a shared geography of the Sacred, as epitomised in Sinai and Jerusalem. If we can strive jointly to recover the Sense of the Sacred, there are many areas in which we can move forward with mutual respect, and to great mutual advantage. And if we succeed in the effort, God willing, the reward is peace and harmony in our inner selves, and within and between our different cultures and societies.

3   Summary of Discussion

Several noteworthy points, described as a 'cascade of ideas', were made during a 30 minute discussion following the presentations by the speakers:

1. There was much support for the re-integration of sacred elements of life into areas where they had been 'removed'. Religion had retreated from the public world. Retrieving some of the 'baby and the bathwater' would be hugely beneficial, particularly if traditional concepts and principles could be moulded into the contemporary. Undertaking a critique of traditions should be done as an inter-faith exercise.

2. Sharing a return to a Sense of the Sacred should be achieved through a multi-dimensional approach which would strengthen dialogue between the West and Islam, and between the West and all Eastern faiths. The language of spirituality and the language of art are 'common denomi-

nators'. Discussions between the West and Islam tended to be temporal and become a 'dialogue of the deaf' over such issues as human rights, democracy and fundamentalism. Dialogue about the Sacred in different cultures, about shared beliefs of love, tolerance and faith in God, could strengthen understanding between faiths.

3. Given our common citizenship of earth, it is necessary to build more bridges through multi-cultural, multinational and multi-religious means, in a search for unity.

4. Science, traditionally a bridge between cultures in different times, should be a meeting place between different religions. In the West, God had been expelled from the laboratories— science is often seen as an enemy of religion. Scientific and technological revolutions cannot be reversed yet there could be a humble willingness for religion to confess 'honest failure'.

5. A rediscovery of the spiritual could help us to understand and to improve management of the planet. Environmental and scientific issues are sometimes thinly veiled surrogates for the failure of mankind to resolve more fundamental issues such as a 'just' resource distribution, and a common respect for people. The spirit of Assisi could help groups work for common goals. The Millennium could help change the Western environmental agenda in a positive way.

6. An inter-faith approach, would lead to a more holistic approach in healthcare, and other social areas.

7. Scientific discovery and exploring the material world should be passed on to children with a spiritual dimension. Children should also be taught to look at religion from the point of view of imagination.

8. Examining Western democracy and *Shariah* law more profoundly would be beneficial as there are many similarities between them.

List of Participants

HRH THE PRINCE OF WALES: St James's Palace, London
ADAMSON, Hugh: Baha'i Community of the UK, London
AL-DUWAISAN, Khalid: Embassy of the State of Kuwait, London
AL-GURG, Easa Saleh: Embassy of United Arab Emirates, London
AL-KHOEI, Yousif: Al-Khoei Foundation, London
AL-MAJED, Hamad: London Central Mosque and Islamic
  Cultural Centre, London
ALGOSAIBI, Ghazi: Royal Embassy of Saudi Arabia, London
ALI, A H Mahmood: Bangladesh High Commission, London
ARCHIBALD, Liliana: Wilton Park Academic Council, London
ARMSTRONG, Karen: Writer and Broadcaster, London
BADAWI, Mohamed Zaki: The Muslim College, London
BARRINGTON-WARD, Simon: The Lord Bishop of Coventry
BATTISCOMBE, Christopher: Foreign and Commonwealth
  Office, London
BRADLEY, Stephen: Foreign and Commonwealth Office, London
BROWNING, David: Oxford Centre for Islamic Studies, Oxford
BREHONY, John: Rolls-Royce plc, London
BUTT, Nasim: King Fahad Academy, London
CALDICOTT, Fiona: Somerville College, Oxford
COLES, John: Foreign and Commonwealth Office, London
CRAIG, James: Middle East Association, London
CRITCHLOW, Keith: The Prince of Wales Institute of
  Architecture, London
CROWE, Virginia: Wilton Park, Steyning
DAOUD, Azzam: Embassy of the Hashemite Kingdom of Jordan,
  London
DENTON, Geoffrey: Federal Trust, London
EATON, Charles Le Gai: Islamic Cultural Centre, London
FISK, David: Department of the Environment, London
GLEDHILL, Ruth: "The Times", London
GORING, Harry: Wiston Estate Office, Steyning
HADDAOUI, Khalil: Embassy of the Kingdom of Morocco,
  London
HART, Robin: Wilton Park, Steyning
HOPKINSON, Nicholas: Wilton Park, Steyning

JAHANPOUR, Farhang: Department for Continuing Education, Oxford

JENNINGS, Colin: Director and Chief Executive, Wilton Park, Steyning

KABBANI, Rana: Writer, London

KAMARUDIN, Dato: Malaysian High Commission, London

KASER, Michael: The Sir Heinz Koeppler Trust, Oxford

KNIGHT, John: High Sheriff of West Sussex, Arundel

LAMB, Christopher: Council of Churches for Britain and Ireland, London

LAMPORT, Stephen: St James's Palace, London

LATTER, Richard: Wilton Park, Steyning

LESLIE, Mariot: Foreign and Commonwealth Office, London

LITTLE, Jenny: Wilton Park, Steyning

LONGLEY, Clifford: Journalist, Orpington

MALCOLM, Jim: Foreign and Commonwealth Office, London

MARSH, Richard: The Archbishop of Canterbury's Secretary for Ecumenical Affairs

MUNRO, Alan: Former British Ambassador to Saudi Arabia and Algeria, London

NAIM, Moeen: High Commission for The Islamic Republic of Pakistan, London

NAZIR-ALI, Michael: Bishop of Rochester

NEUBERGER, Julia: Rabbi, London

NIBLOCK, Timothy: University of Durham

NICHOLSON, Emma: House of Commons, London

NIZAMI, Fahan: Director, Oxford Centre for Islamic Studies, Oxford

PALMER, Martin: International Consultancy on Religion, Education and Culture, Manchester Metropolitan University

PEACOCKE, Arthur: Oxford University, Oxford

POLKINGHORNE, John: Fellow and Former President, Queens' College, Cambridge

QUINLAN, Michael: Ditchley Park, Enstone

RAFIQ, Bashir: Ahmadiyya Muslim Association, London

RINPOCHE, Chime: The Tibetan Buddhist Centre, Ashdon

ROGALY, Joseph: "Financial Times", London

ROWE, Caroline: Home Office, London

SANBERK, Özdem: Turkish Embassy, London

SAYYAR, Waheed: Embassy of the State of Bahrain, London
SCHIMMEL, Annemarie: Professor Emerita, Universities of Harvard and Bonn
SHAKER, Mohamed: Embassy of the Arab Republic of Egypt, London
SHEPHERD, John: Foreign and Commonwealth Office, London
SINGHVI, Laxmi: High Commission of India, London
VAUGHAN, Philippa: The Royal Asiatic Society, London
WARD, Philip: Her Majesty's Lord Lieutenant for West Sussex, Arundel
WITTON, Trevor: British Petroleum plc, London

Printed in the United Kingdom for The Stationery Office
J33003 C3 1/98 10170